LM

CLUELESS DOGS

for Blake

CLUELESS DOGS

RHIAN EDWARDS

SEREN

Seren is the book imprint of
Poetry Wales Press Ltd.
57 Nolton Street, Bridgend, Wales, CF31 3AE

www.serenbooks.com
Facebook: facebook.com/SerenBooks
Twitter: @SerenBooks

ISBN: 978-1-85411-573-7
e-pub: 978-1-85411-595-9
Kindle 978-1-78172-000-4

A CIP record for this title is available from the British Library.

The publisher acknowledges the financial assistance of the Welsh Books
Council.

Cover art:'On the Spot' by Peter Clark: www.peterclarkcollage.com

Printed in Bembo by The Grosvenor Group (Print Services) London Ltd

Author's weblinks: www.rhianedwards.co.uk
www.myspace.com/rianedwards
www.myspace.com/rhianedwardsmusic

Contents

I

II

Parents' Evening

We feel she may be cheating
at reading and spelling.
She has failed to grasp the planets
and the laws of science,
has proven violent in games
and fakes asthma for attention.

She is showing promise with the Odyssey,
has learned to darn starfish
and knitted a patch for the scarecrow.
She seems to enjoy measuring rain,
pretending her father is a Beatle
and insists upon your death
as the conclusion to all her stories.

The Hatching

Born in the airing cupboard
to the mothering pulse of the boiler,
something cracked its own code
to unearth a second darkness,
a suddenness of space
greater than itself.

Perched on a pyramid
of folded towels and flannels
and crowned in the fragments
of its quondam world,
the fledgling broke into ugly song,
scissoring its beak at the bars
of a wooden planked sky.

The Petrifying Well

We lowered ourselves
into the petrifying well
where lime turned top hats
and bird's nests to stone
and the copper wishing coins
were furring to grey.

We slid on the sediment
of wet currency
as we filled our pockets
with the weight of dead wishes.
The water bleached us –
fossilised our futures –
making rocks of our boredom.

Sick Bed

It went as far as the eyes, stirred
something up, stitching them shut.

The morning I woke to the immediate black,
eyelids padlocked, I howled for myself,

but the tears had nowhere to go, they stayed put,
dammed up against the thin walls of skin.

In the blacked-out room, you let
me lie on you again.

You dabbed and circled pink ointment
into the mohair itch of my body,

while I wriggled, sickened most
at being put back in nappies.

You touched my cheek and palms
with the cool plastic of toys.

I heard you in the doorway, watching
with your hand on your hip.

You did the crying for me,
smoking cigarettes in prayer.

Broken Lifeboat

Mother sleeps foetal in the hollow
of the blue Chesterfield. Praying hands
tucked between her corduroy thighs,
she scowls at her dreams.

I climb the arm of the couch, careful
in a way that is not child-like,
lowering myself into the berth,
the fortified nook behind her legs.

My toy daughters and I are adrift
on a broken lifeboat in a carpet ocean.
Mother is ill and close to death.
Pillow sharks lie in wait.

In whispers, my plot is played out.
My dolls die of starvation.
I hum to them, cradling their lifeless
bodies to my unstarted breast.

Playing Dead

I sucked hold of my breath
for the trick of a noiseless heart.
Head cocked, eyes shut,
mouth ever so slight, I directed
myself into an elegant infant death,
apparently without cause.
I pictured you shaking me,
putting your ear to my chest,
making the screams you never should.

The moment you gave up on me,
I planned to flutter back to life,
rubbing my eyes with my fists,
whispering your favourite name as reward.
After all, my short-lived death
was punishment enough
for ignoring me in the back
with only the occasional glance
in the rear-view mirror.
I carried on dying for years.
You were glad of the silence.

Bridgend

The children are dropping like flies
in my hometown. Nineteen suicides
in no time at all. Nana would have called it
a Biblical curse. Others are guessing
it's some kind of fashion
and hanging is all the rage.
Except for the boy from B&Q,
who tied some rope to a lamppost
got into his car
and pressed down the accelerator.
A work mate found him.
He had his seat belt on,
his head had tumbled to his feet.

My father complains they only parade
the ugly side of his town.
"Why don't they show the stepping stones,
the castle or Southerndown beach?"
But then, Southerndown has been crowned
the third most popular suicide site in Britain.
Cliffs like headstones for giants!
The Samaritans have been lobbying the Vale
for years for a phone box
with a direct dial to a volunteer.
Eventually, the council surrendered and built
the box at the foot of the cliff.

Going Back for Light

Got blacklisted at the colliery for making ructions.
They made him sink too deep and those pocketed
gases got the better. "Nothing like being in hell
with the sky raining rocks at you."
His coughs had been turning red for a while mind.

Explosion lost him a lung and some stomach.
Can't complain though, got him the compo,
couldn't have bought the dance hall without it.
Loved that dance hall, he did. Even laid down
the boards with his own bare hands.

Had to gut the Caerphilly Hall to get that sprung floor.
Beryl had the shock of her life
when she saw Danny leaving, fag in mouth,
a broken-up dance floor under his arm.
Always smoking he was, even with that lonely lung.

You'd have thought there was something missing
from that face if smoke weren't spilling out of it.
Even when he shaved, there it was, cigarette
wagging at his reflection and him scraping the blade
all round it. Getting ready for no good, we reckoned.

"Where you off to Dan?" Edith would ask.
"Going back for light," he'd answer to the mirror.
Never one for talking much. Didn't have to,
what with that smile and those eyes of his.
Pair of chocolates, those eyes.

Daft over him, women were. His dark looks that was,
mind, and him being miner turned ballroom dancer,
moving like milk being poured into a glass.
Threw everyone when he married Edith,
not the prettiest creature but smart as a whip,

everyday studying the *Times* from cover to cover.
Good chapel girl see, never smoked, never drank
never smiled unless she had to. Crossed the room
to stir his tea if he told her.
Danny got all sick and had to give up the fags.

Took up Rolos and peppermints instead, kept boxes of them.
Always something rolling round in his mouth,
never words though, not till he started dying proper
and we got into a halo round his armchair,
tobacco tin on his lap, his old face back.

The Welshman Who Couldn't Sing

I'm sketching his sound;
a motorbike's rumble
or the cartoon voice
of an elderly sheepdog.
The Welshman who couldn't sing,
who could massacre a funeral hymn
with a throatful of catarrh
and a hiccup-spit of words,
a never-ending baffle
to the women of his making.

I'm scratching off a smile
on a weathered, beetroot face.
His Brillo-padded cheeks
could scour skin off my pecking lips
and a yellowing snigger
that thawed me to tears.

I'm mimicking his canon now;
food was his Bible.
With lamb chop in his clutches,
he purred with every gnaw,
his podgy pygmy fingers,
dripping thick in minted gravy,
would wriggle in the supper air
as if knitting a potent sentence.

I'm fattening up his bones
to a torso like a turnip.
A hill of hairless belly
I climbed and conquered as a baby
and a spooned-out pit of navel
that could house an old ten-penny.

I'm giving back his limbs
two arms wooden to the hip,
sleeves of freckles to the knuckle,
fingers curled in threatless fists.
His gypsy-dog thin legs
marched with the scurries
of an unleashed toddler,
forever, it seems, betraying
the weight he was made to haul.

House Key

Your mother climbed the driveway,
found you playing marbles
on the doorstep, singing to yourself.
You knew full well to post
your hand through the letterbox,
grab the latchkey on the string
and let yourself in. You elected
to be shut out, petrified
a house without people
could swallow or erase you.

You now pace your front lawn,
the self-made man, the seller
of houses. You light cigarettes
and flick them away, kick up
the flowers, punishing them
for their idleness, your wife's
truancy, her unmentioned absence.

You prod the doorbell in provocation,
choking your home with a chronic
merry-go-round chime. You spy
through the eyelid of the letter box,
patrol the outside walls like a wolf.
Your family remains unconjured.
Your house keys spill over
the lip of your trouser pocket,
as you tremble in wait in the car.

Traveller

The crooked stem of the driveway
and the terracotta jigsaw
of the flower pots you've run over,
are the last leg of this journey home
to find you tucked inside a frame
of French windows, slumped and stolid,
head bowed to your chest.

Even dead to the world, you clutch
fast to your glass of red,
the sleeping knight's hand
knows peace on the hilt of his sword.
You are blue-bleached as a statue
in the grasping flickers of the television,
staunch and untouched
by my locked-out calls,
my knuckles beating on glass.

Rhys

Like the time you invited me inside
the ottoman on the landing
and sat on the lid laughing
while I scratched and screamed at the wood.

Or when the babysitter wasn't looking,
you taught me the quickest way to add nine,
showed me to tie my laces with the tale
of two rabbits disappearing down a hole.

Like the day you caught the slow-worm
that tried to whip away the sun,
letting it loose into the folds
of the blanket that I held like a lover.

Not to mention the crimes I invented
for which I never knew you were beaten,
or that summer you took away the stabilisers
to be the sole witness to me riding away.

Like the times I spied in your bedroom,
played your records and fanned open your books,
only to slip between the sheets
with a nakedness meant only for bath time.

Camposuil

From a verse pattern originated at Tŷ Newydd, 2010.

Remember when my sunburn roared like nettle rash
and the daisies died as soon as they were chained?

And when we balanced on the sewage pipe that bridged the Ogwr
and rode the river in the rubber ring of a lorry tyre?

Or in Cefn Glas, when Charlotte from the council estate
got the puppies to lick Monster Munch off her tongue?

Don't tell me you don't remember necking Shandy
on the roundabout that nearly killed you?

Or when we watched the babysitter get shagged,
balls of socks in our gobs and we still fell apart.

And the school holiday we played knock-a-door-run
and you poured boiling water on my second degree sunburn?

No Place

Painted roses and ivy scratch
a tangled stairway up the wall.
They twist an arch around a false
front door, sealed before it learned.
The windows are criss-crossed
clown eyes, paneless frames
shedding black silence.

Unhook the face of the house,
peel it open like a page,
every room surrenders itself,
perfectly furnished for no one.
A tall lamp mourns an unused
armchair, a hat stand presides
in the corner like a winter tree.

My hand is the ghost and god
of this home. Fingers drift –
intent for the solid, skate over
the hexagonal table, the velvet
dining room chairs, roll back
the eyelid of the bureau,
pinch open famished drawers.

Fingers scramble through a hatch
into a mock mahogany bedroom –
where the wardrobe is cluttered
with air and the mirror has forgotten
how to watch. The hand pauses –
shrinks from a familiar bed
where a spider closes into a fist.

Unmentionable

He rusts my blood,
cadavers my skin,
sweating a smile,
a jaundice-licked grin.

Hid, curled and trembling,
my eyes sealed to blind,
a mock of saliva
scratches teeth down my spine.

While a nocturne of moths
bat their wings in my belly,
my heart, red and fisted,
thumps its cage to betray me.

Please hush now this heart
to dumben this breath,
muffle the whimpers,
the drippings of sweat.

Claw back the tears
and gnaw off this tongue,
unquiver the jaw
caesura this lung.

Die me a death
To deprive me of sense,
maim me or sleep me,
let the horror be silenced.

Ritual

He kept brushing her hair
for longer than he needed to –
lost in the ritual
of dragging boar bristles
across her small scalp,
stroking slow to the tips.

The knots had been corrected
and the tangles taught to behave
long before. She anchors
her stare at the table's edge.
He makes a leash out of auburn.

Steed

Olive-green skulled, an upside down
eye, a broom for a body,
a wooden wheel for a hoof,
you were my beast, my favourite,
my nameless toy. Between the podge
of my thighs, you were my partner in crime.
Together we galloped through rooms
and gymkhanaed the chairs,
I fed you dandelions and bog water,
rammed your muzzle into walls.

Now you lean your punch-drunk head
against the fire's mantle.
Crowned in a silver cloche hat,
noosed in an ostrich feather boa,
you are dandified, moribund,
a Rosebud, a relic
put out to pasture, living
proof we were once something else.

Polly

The gap between your teeth became my ambition,
as did your bias for fountain pens,
rubbing your nose with the ball
of your hand. That succession of clicks
where the bone seemingly turned.
I always wondered at the violence
you gave your cropped hair, yanking a fistful
of it down to your shoulder, a modest trick,
the pretence of decrying yourself
while delivering a lavish answer.

I secretly warred with you in French
and English though never destined
to beat you. Still, we were able to share
the teacher we loved and code-named
Cornelius, as we watched him on Fridays,
buy flowers at the bus station.
We both lived for the pauses
where we composed ghost stories
for each other, promenading the playground,
our arms linked and unbreakable.

How I admired the mess you made,
your massacre of books, the pencilled
note at your bedside, toasting you
for completing *War and Peace*
by the age of eleven. What I wouldn't
have given for your attic scatter,
the names of your sisters,
your fountain pen handwriting, the turgid
lettering I mimicked in secret
and now pass off as my own.

Petra

Remember when Tommo found the library
and fingered out that Blue Peter classic
Petra: A Dog For All Seasons?
That title clung to you like a Kick Me sign
sticky-taped to the back of your blazer.

You took your pseudonym well,
stormed the school like Boudicca –
all matronly bounce and mucky blonde hair,
a dirty fat smile for the corridors
and purple Doc Martens Tippexed with stars.

Both your parents were vicars,
built like polar bears and born in their cardigans.
They let you say *fucking* before everything,
Even blessed you with the biggest room in the vicarage.
And you got your own kettle and teabags,
which made you practically an adult.

But how did you sleep in that room, Petra Hawksworth,
amongst the spread-eagled sheet music,
the straggle of elephantine bras
and unwanted pants that puddled the floor?
It was a wonder you could revise
in the thick of your circus of gay porn pinups
chewing-gum-tacked to the walls.

Remember the night of the harvest festival
when your soprano solo made the music teacher weep?
At David Newman's party at his father's hotel,
you came into your own,
realised the Petra you hankered for.

That was the night your boobs came out to play.
You got off with the room, snog-hacked
a thoroughfare from kitchen to lounge.
You fell to your knees in the garden
and in the cold grass earned your fellatio wings.

Alison

The day is frayed and it's barely begun.
Mind, I've been picking at the thread,
unribboning the weft
with a long-drawn out sigh.
The office rolls its eye.

Tanya is flapping again,
her daughter keeps nicking her fags
and trampolining the dog till its sick.
No time for coffee, I scold her for asking.
The phone bleats from my handbag.

Somebody's fucked up somewhere,
I don't know where but I'll find out,
I'll give that girl hell now,
gave me the wrong bloody keys, didn't she.
My head's in the shed again.

Isn't anyone going to answer that?!
I swanky my voice for the phone
by not moving my lips. Where did my lips go?
Been saying his name without thinking
for thirty years. I knife through the mail.

Penetrative Discourse

i.m. Dorothy Parker, 1893-1967

Tonight my rhetoric is running on empty.
Well to be perfectly honest, it ain't
running at all. Instead it's nursing
inebria and candid remarks,
irresponsibly imparted the night before.
Tonight I'm all out of my idiolect
and my signature wit, yet you still hang
on my every like a chimp on a twig.
I mean look at you.

On the edge of your seat, metaphorical
of course, impatiently awaiting
some sardonic retort. What is this
conversation to you anyway? Repartee
tennis or a derisory blood sport?
Feeling unindulged now are we? Deflated
by a distinct absence of eloquence?
Well I've done my hard time,
I've completed my sentence.

Ghost Water

You hatched into flower,
clung to a dead thing,
the indifferent rock.

In adult medusa you uprooted, became
a wandering lamp, an indolent disciple
of the currents that fetched for you.

You never thought to swim
in a sea that was intent
upon starving you, hustling you
into the deadest of pools

You chased the arc of the sun
and learned to lap up
the sugars of your parasites.

In ghost water you thrived,
billowed into a smothering
patchwork, a virus of light.

Outcast Hours

White light weighs heavy, bullying
bright as squash courts. I fix a dirty look
on the electric clock. The walled
minutes stagger their blinks.

Wheel-footed suitcases scurry
about me like clueless dogs,
flip flops tick-tock
on the polished rink of the concourse.

One girl's patience is vivid,
measured by the careful brush strokes
of plum on her toenails,
the soft turning of pages.

Her boyfriend hibernates,
his legs stretched out before him.
Ankles crossed, he wags his foot
conducting his concert of sleep.

A ponytailed mother raises
an eye for her wandering son.
She scoops him up and breathes in his scalp
in chase of a smell that is running away from her.

The antique couple are butchering time.
Their teeth tear through baguettes
raining faded confetti
onto their open laps.

Shy of games and companions, fidgeting
in plastic-boned chairs, we comb the air
for that splintered voice,
dictating when our sky will ship us.

Strangers

are for remembering
how a mouth works,
the liquid shapes,
the gurn of a kiss.

The mind can't help
but narrate the action
of an imprecise hand
finding its way about you.

★

Eyeful

Looking me dizzy
licking me drunk
in the face of our nudity
I am not nearly naked enough

Sea of Her

Head pillowed on belly
of vanilla-soaked flesh,
this skull rowed her gently
to her lappings of breath.

There, I dozed and I dreamed,
I lazed and I lounged.
In her pool of milk skin
this man practically drowned.

★

After

I empty my room of last night.
I tread barefoot about the house,
open every window, telling
myself I'm airing the place.

I fill up the kettle, forget
what for and wander away
to find myself in a mirror
looking for something to pluck.

Skype

for B.L.H.

Now we have fallen by way
of a window, the motion
picture of a mouth, the faithful
companion of the voice,
staggered by a split
second.

Now we can only see the other
by looking away from the lens,
the voyeur conversing
with its prey,
caressing your face
with a cursor.

Now we have come to a blur,
a pixelated mashing of atoms,
stock-stilled in vignette,
we re-focus the cynosure
with the fractious waking
of a bleary eye.

Now we are a screen, a sea
apart. Three thousand miles
as the crow flies, you lean
in for the kiss with only
the blue iris of the camera
to requite it.

Quotidian

It's all about the habits –
pick-pocketing five more minutes
from a clock that rolls its eye
and buries its head in the pillow.

It's all about those minutes –
lips stepping the stones of your spine,
the banshee of an alarm
that brings us back to our senses.

It's all about disarray –
coffee pot wobbling on the gas hob,
black liquid spitting at the kitchen tiling,
toothpaste bearding my chin.

It's all about the hush –
laying the mug beside you,
you mumbling the dearest of thank-yous
for a drink you're unlikely to touch.

Gravy

We rock like a crib in a book –
crowded room to pictures of your wife
grinning through the ages.

You call me 'darling' and I stifle
a giggle. It's all a bit cloying
and anxious, you and me.

You start to sweat. It smells
of gravy. And wanting to be
myself, I tell you.

Back to Bed

You rip off the blankets
to stop me losing the day.
I dream in epics, you see.
Sometimes you think I won't wake
and might adventure without you.

I'm a drawer fully open
now something has to be touched.
You list my bits that you prize,
lower a kiss to the belly.
What a waste of good fawning
when the flattered is sleep-swooned!

Instead it's the chill of your spit
and the wind you've let in
that shudder me back to the room
and this ordinary morning –
all thumping in sunshine
which I wish I could bin.

I abandon your bed for the bathroom
and the griffin-clawed tub,
which squats under the window,
cupping the punctured clouds
of your lather.

I pussy-foot into the tepid.
The yellowed porcelain squeaks as I slide.
I wheel the hot tap with my toe,
veil my face in damp flannels
and in the snug of the soap-swamp,
perfect my vanishing act.

The Action

This window is my television
the action is slight –
blue pieces of sky trawl through the grey.

A crow scribbles a diagonal
erasing its script with each wing beat,
bee-humming engines prowl beneath me.

Toyed by the wind, a telephone wire
trembles like a tightrope
after the walker has leapt.

Old Friends

I blink dumbfounded from bed
as you parade jumpers on hangers.

You look from one to the other
like they were ghosts of old friends.

Yet they've been rotting without you,
moth-picnicked to tatters.

It's sweet you still care
now the outside hardly sees you

and here you are knitting your brows
between two different rags.

Safe

for M.H.

We're turning into serious
drinkers for each other.
At least shyness won't bother us
as we spill into ourselves.

I'm coming to rely on the stories
you never remember
and the mantra of nodding
at your rambunctious promises.

The adventure is dulling.
Safe in the little harms I do,
I rehearse permutations of futures
where I dare to be certain of you.

The Wrong Season

The wasp nest ruptured that winter,
the week I helped myself to your address,
convinced you it was the best thing for us.

It was just their corpses at first,
strewn across carpets, the tops of books,
blackened and curled like burnt matches.

Live ones followed, drunk on the wrong season,
sluggishly crawling the panes, dragging
their signatures through the bath-steamed window.

They put their minds to the condensation,
caught a peepshow of the familiar
and head-butted the trick of glass.

A few became shadow puppets of themselves,
trapped behind the bedroom blind,
zombie-chanting their morning song.

One bleary wasp had the gumption for flight,
tightroped the Christmas card string, caught
fluff on its tail, a shabby bridal train.

Crossed

She wears her head
on the bone of his shoulder,
wraps his cold hand
in the skin of her own.

He doesn't unfold
or relent an affection,
just parks a white gaze
in the humdrum of windows.

She noses his neck,
pretends pretty sleep,
he keeps his limbs crossed,
his eyelids unbatted.

He ghosts the girl,
forgetting to want her,
as she knits a clement world
around his unwanting.

Marital Visit

for H.W.

It's her visiting time
which presses the pause,
makes you follow me downstairs
and shepherd me out of the door.

I sigh the train South,
unearth my unwanted habits,
remind all my rooms
to smell of me again.

Like the man who threw a party
but didn't dare touch a drop,
you busy yourself in the tidying,
the rounding up of my scraps.

The ritual begins with the clearing
away of my face: foundation, lipstick,
powder, concealer, the wooden brush
cobwebbed with my unyielding knots.

Everything strewn like toys on the surface
of her kidney-shaped dressing table,
is gathered and bagged as on the day
they had the nerve to arrive.

You empty the shelves of my skin:
the eczema ointments, the bottled fake tan,
the perfume you bought on a whim
that patched me in rashes.

Flicked over the edge,
my pieces topple into the dark of the bag,
where they chink together
as if to toast their reunion.

Your wife lets herself in,
carries herself across the threshold,
she smiles at her hallway,
sniffing me everywhere.

Suitcase

A ventriloquist's doll
dangling limbs, a fixed
laughing grin, unable to talk back,

unable to blink without
the perch of your knee.
You fold me in at the waist,

my feet kicking my ears,
squeezed in a suitcase
and shelved out of sight

till I wake to the rattling,
the sound of your wife hanging
her blouses beneath me.

Fruition

Ripe is the night
to sever our hips,
to unfurl the locked fingers
and unbuckle the kiss.

Ripe is this night
to come clean and confess,
to unshoulder the burden,
admit we want more than
this fruition of boredom,
the equation of us.

Ripe is the night
to let lips re-acquaint,
to talk in nostalgias,
exhuming *I love you's,*
sandwiched in sheets
and cwtched under covers,
resuming our throne
as the meant-to-be lovers,

Will the night ever ripen
to slice us in two?
When the kisses core hollow
and the mattress sags sallow,
when the sleep of your face
is decrowned of a halo.

Ripe will that night be
to rip up the twinning
and become whole as a half,
leaving love and its tedium.

Hitched

Violent tiredness has stripped
our mouths down to skeletal
talk and a grimacing silence.

These tongues that once swaggered
with muscles of mirth, now flap
at the table, starved of all rapture.

In a bootless attempt to replenish
lost joys, you pluck from the napkin
a tale for the telling.

With a flurry of arm wags and plasticine
face, you spill all the beans
for a flicker of awe.

I dispatch a dim smile and spy
on the gossips, as the swelling dead air
rots the menu between us.

Hunch

My mouth has been falling to pieces again.
I've been Sellotaping the faults,
making a blur of conversations,
drawing lines where they should be.

The hunch has come crawling back.
Is it because I've been living in my throat
and trembling at every kindness?
One day I'll cry and make a sound.

I'm procrastinating in the bathroom again,
shirking the relentless constant of bedtime
where you will be patient or cruel. Can I
get up now, even though it's still dark?

Coldsores

The worry spoils, blistering
my mouth with coldsores. They cling
for dear life, feeding
like acorn barnacles chewing
the hide of a whale.

We falter down Camden Passage
through the swell of the Easter mob.
They catch peeks of my cauliflower lip
and reckon me some kind of filth
or swollen with husbandly punches.

I smear on the ointment, becoming
a freak-show of a white-moustached lady,
still the virus fidgets,
itching to spread, pulsing avid
as a stripped heart on display.

Our slow marches arrive us too soon,
sheltered in the Angel station.
Unable to kiss now, we block
the turnstile with our thin goodbye,
getting in the way of the weekend's escape.

You dress the bag round my shoulders,
peck me on the forehead as you would
a daughter at bedtime.
I try a smile, which fractures
the sores, making my mouth bleed.

Pinchbeck

The house is a counterfeit of itself.
The kitchen keeps scouring
the surfaces and the crockery is forever
getting soiled and plunging
in and out of the basin. Different tea bags
press against the window of the jar.

The tangerine tablecloth has buckled
under the strain, folded into
a fraction of itself and gone
into hiding in the charity bag.
A plastic square lies sprawled in its place,
a lilac cartoon of flying cups and saucers.

It seems the basement study has let itself go,
got into a scrap with your papers,
left the drawers gasping for air.
You can't blame it really. What with only
a slit of garden to look at. It's a wonder
a word was ever penned here.

Your bedroom has lost its bottles.
There are no trinkets scattered
around the mirror and no face powder
dusting the wood. Her hanging rail
has been picked to the bones
and wears only the white wall behind it.

The Good Hand

You can't remember exactly when
the house turned against you,
why it pushed you down the stairs,
stabbed you in the hand
and left cancers strewn about.

You were dozing when it happened,
cradling your arm like a lamb,
when they came in through the skylight,
in whispers at first: a mob
of voices circling you like flies.

You tried locking them in,
but the key wouldn't listen.
It sliced your good hand to ribbons,
leaving you to war with the door
and the frantic twists from the other side.

Nyctophobia

It is the darkness between rooms
you have to look out for,
the scorched blur in the corner
that comes crouching up to you.
It is remembering to flick the switch
before you cross the brink, pausing
till the bulb has caught up
and the air has stopped moving.
Never set foot into the black;
disinfect each room with light.

Do not take the dark for granted.
It does not belong to you. Not here,
where the seconds stretch into a scar
and the room plays Grandmother's Footsteps
until you dare not look away. Be wary
of the silences, the biding of time.
Brim the house with voices: your own,
television, radio, a mimicked conversation,
anything to smother the tongues,
the scattering of marbles above you.

Shardeloes Road

It is not the long dressing gown
hanging from the hook
drifting towards the bed,

not the bra slung over the chair,
its Siamese twinned cups
shining like the scalps of babies.

It is not the shuffling of cards
beneath the bed, the whisperings, the white spider
disappearing into the grain of the drawer.

It is not this room's countless faces
that make this sleep brittle and unsafe
and keep me pawing at the air for the light.

No. It is the blanket that buries
and surrounds me that has suddenly taken
to breathing in spite of me.

The Woman Downstairs

She stalks my nightly footsteps
with the syncopated thump of a broom
slips folded notes under the door

claiming my television's mutterings
come to her like schizophrenia
my slippered treads are a dead body

in a trunk being dragged across the room
my tender tapping of poems are nothing
but a twisted take on water-torture.

Skeeter Syndrome

I felt a tickle to my ankle,
saw her, dithering in the air
light as dandelion snow,
a winged needle, a mother-to-be
clumsy with the harvest of my blood.

I caught her dancing on the wall,
crushed her with a single applaud.
I opened my hand to a mangle of limbs,
a patch of my own blood - the stigma
of killing something full of me.

The Unkindness

The unkindness of flesh as it drifts
from the bone. Where the lithe
has melted into a cosy body,
plump-pillowed, an armchair for sleeping.
The skin is gathered in fistfuls,
stuffed, unemptyable pockets,
dough ripe for the kneading.
I sway the swinging bridge
of the underarm, cling to the fat
that garlands my spine.

Explain these dog-eared breasts,
the widening canyon at their root,
the browned nipple that has become
their conclusion? See these hips
scored with the Chinese burns
of dereliction and a mother's billowing.
What of this cauliflowering arse,
where are the buttocks that snake charmed?
Riddle me this that has fallen
and lumbers in my hands.

Sheer

Like a crack in the egg,
a lash in the eye,
a smattering of black grass
marring the blanch of the moon,

black hairs spear through the pale
pink wheel of my nipple,
whisker-thick to the pinch,
sprouting sheer as a thorn.

Perhaps it is the fray
from the seams of my skin,
a rag doll unstitching
her two needless patches.

Eight threads puncture the thin
limpid membrane of halo.
This breast is gravid
with a hatching of spiders.

Tiptoe

I wander dreamless through your dialogues,
the ephemera of affection.
I traipse shoeless through these dialects,
these contentious claims to passions.

I pressed these brittle soles
upon the fire-licked blistered coals,
upon the stain that broke the glass,
the egg-shells and kid gloves
and through the splinters, flints and shards,
I forged these uneroded paths.

Yet I tiptoe though your daydreams,
the outcast to your trances toyed at night.
Meanwhile, buoyed by moons and frozen sheets,
I thumped the thinning ice.

Now I meander through the arid,
abandoning lands where I've expired
I'm walking dead to you, bereft of you,
with crumbs of poems left of you,
armed with a memory now for forgetting you.

So I wander seamless through this monologue,
my forever of affection.
I traipse boot-laced in my idiolect,
my unchampioned claims to passions.

For you may tear this infrastructure,
this composure cannot flounder,
armed with the toughness of magnolia,
the cold robustness of a character
that seems to make and merit me
as my mother's God-damned daughter.

For I'm my walker, I'm my soldier,
I'm my legion and stigmata
and with the foot-bind of a concubine,
I'll still march on and over.
For there's no man, no situation
worth the shame to ever crawl for.

And yet I tiptoe through your daydreams.
Still I tiptoe through your daydreams.

And when that thought has passed,
have I left my mark?
Not even a foot print
of me now remains.

Pest Controller

My offer of tea was cryptic code
for marriage. He politely declined,
obliging me to make small talk
about infestations. I showed him the oven,
where I accidentally roasted a mouse
and told him I drowned one in a bin
when I caught it pissing blood.

Another one came to my bedroom to die.
I explained I wrote poems to excuse
my bedlam hair, ramshackle clobber
and foul play with rodents.
What kind of stuff do you write? He asked,
sticking his head in the bathroom cupboard
while fiddling for daydreaming vermin.

Love poems, the dark side, I said
hounding him round the house, wondering
whether to give him a dedicated
copy of my book or slap on some face.
Then you don't know what love is, he said,
shaking poisoned grain into boxes
as if he were emptying a sweet jar.

Girl Meats Boy

The goose-necked fork and the cat-fanged knife
stood poles apart, like soldiering guards,
west and easting a world of plate
of petticoat white,
piled mole-mound high,
with the tatters of a man,
who had recently expired.

And my fingers thimbled fish cold steel,
eyes plump as fruit, with dripping pout,
my tongue unrolled red carpet-like,
as I ploughed and trowelled with tools and cut.

For plattered here was my better half,
my all-consuming light and dark,
who saw us better as separate halves.
A divorce I decreed with a slit apart.

And his white neck smirked an angry grin,
as the liquid poured in beetroot red.
Berry tears stained wall and tile,
as he stagger-waltzed, while draining dead.

He rag-doll slumped in a choir of pans,
where stew pots stooled his skull.
And all was mute, 'cept weep of wound
ink-blotting troughs of metal.

I heaved the stew pots, bucket-brimmed,
slammed down on hobs and flame,
and fried the blood fat, pudding-black,
a macabre supper entertained.

Slabbed flat on ground, I sponged him down,
combed clean of smear and dirt.
I raked off hair with scrape and pluck
and skinned him pink and bald as birth.

I butchered limbs with rabid zeal
and knifed through muscled plums.
I ripped and gutted, as he did me,
and reduced this man to crumbs.

Ginger-root doused butter sweats
of garlic rocks and peppered dust,
I basted thigh and rump and breast,
and cooked him gold in a parsnipped nest.

His wave of hands slid down in soup
of mushroom nutmeg milk,
so dab of hand and finger-tickle
could brush my lips with each spooned gulp.

I jellied thoughts in pickle sour,
soused face in stew of onions.
I parched his ears to biscuit bread,
crisped nose to pencil shavings.

I cured his heart, I syruped it sweet,
cake-baked in cream and cherries.
My menyou done, I throned to dine,
claw-pawed at the ash grey cutlery.

Lips fell apart for kiss of you,
bled puddled spit for scraps of you,
gouged cheeks of meat to feast on you,
tore threads of flesh in teeth of you,
licked marrow, bone and pulp of you,
let belly swell with fat of you,
pigged pregnant with the pith of you,
gut, liver, spleen digesting you,
my newborn blood absorbing you,
my pulse, my veins, heart pumping you.
No flies on you, no worms in you,
no scavenge bait, no urn of you.

From liver to liver,
heart to heart
blood to blood.

This woman, she made
a meal of you.

Acknowledgements

Are due to the following publications where some of these poems first appeared: *Areté, Borderlines, The Delinquent, Domestic Cherry, The London Magazine, Planet, Poetry London, Pen Pusher, Poetry Review, Poetry Wales, The Raconteur, The Same, The Spectator, Stand, The Times Literary Supplement, The Wolf, The Guardian*, and *The Lampeter Review.*

'Hunch' appeared in *Lung Jazz: The Cinnamon Anthology for Young Poets.*

Parade the Fib, a pamphlet published by Tall Lighthouse, was awarded the Poetry Book Society Pamphlet Choice for Autumn of 2008.

The Poem 'Girl Meats Boy' won both the audience and judges' Award in the John Tripp Spoken Poetry competition in 2011.

The Author wishes to acknowledge the Arts Council of England for the receipt of a bursary to complete this book.

I would like to thank Hugo Williams, Amy Wack and everyone in the editorial attic at Seren, Christopher Reid, Carol Ann Duffy, Gillian Clark, Robert Minhinnick, the faithfully discerning Thurlow Road Poetry Group, Luke and Sally Wright, Les Robinson of Tall Lighthouse, not to mention my dearest friends and muses: Blake Harwell, SP Howarth, Ben Ripley (né Hampson), Clay Fussell, Rob Chandler, Steve Day, Hannah James, Laura Forster, Dinah Roe, Susie Wild, Victoria Humphreys, Tracy Evans, my brothers Lloyd and Rhys, Aunty Lynne, my parents Gareth and Kay and not forgetting the staff at Gareth L Edwards Ltd.